To: ♡

From: χ

To my biggest supporters of
whatever I do in life,
a.k.a
The Knebel Team!

THE LAST TASK

by Cigdem Knebel
Simple Words Books™

FREE DECODABLE
PHONICS WORKBOOK
and
FREE ACCESS TO ONLINE SUMMITS

simplewordsbooks.com

Chapter 1
A Job In Madrid

It is a hot, fall day in West Trent. Tom and Stan sit on the grass. They are best pals.

A big red truck stands on the block. On the front of the truck, it says, "WE GET YOU TO YOUR NEXT STOP."

Stan is sad that the truck has his best pal Tom's stuff in it.

Tom and Stan do not say much. They sit in the sun next to Stan's swing set. But they do not plan to do a thing. They are sad that this is their last day.

The stamp plant in West Trent was shut down last May. All of the plant's staff has lost their jobs.

Stan's dad had a job in the stamp plant and he was let go. He still has no job. West Trent is not that big. With the plant shut down, there are not a lot of jobs left for Stan's dad.

Tom's dad had a job in the plant as well. Stan and Tom's wish was for their dads to get jobs fast. They did not wish the next job for Tom's dad to be in Madrid. But it is.

Tom's dad is Spanish and he got a job in Madrid. Tom will be living there with his mom and dad. They do not plan to be back. Stan will miss Tom a lot.

In the spring, Stan lost his gran, Gran Jenn. She was his dad's mom. Then his dad lost his job. In the fall, his best pal is off to Madrid.

This is a lot for Stan.

Stan sits next to Tom as the men bring out beds, the TV set and a big box with a tag that says, 'Tom's Stuff'.

Tom tells Stan that the men will ship their things all the way past the Atlantic.

"Mom thinks Madrid will be fun," he adds.

Stan stands up. He kicks a rock off the grass and sags.

"Fun or not, I still wish you did not have to go," he grunts.

"I wish to stay with you in West Trent," Tom says. "But it is not up to me."

Chapter 2
A Gift From Tom

At 1 p.m., a cab stops next to the truck. Tom's dad brings out the bags and stuffs them in the trunk of the cab. Tom's mom tells Tom to get in the cab.

Stan's chin drops to his chest.

"You must go!" sniffs Stan.

"Yes. Call me and tell me what I miss in West Trent," Tom says with a half grin.

Stan nods.

"Tom, we are all set," says his dad. "Be quick! We must go if you still plan to..."

"Yes, Dad!" Tom yells in a rush to hush him.

Then, he hugs Stan.

Stan does not let the hug go.

He will not let Tom go.

But Tom steps back. He brings out a black tin chest from his backpack.

He hands it to Stan. "And this, this is for you, if you miss me."

On top of the lid, a red tag says, "To: Stan, From: Tom".

Stan grabs the lid to lift it and check what is in it.

"Not yet," Tom stops Stan.

"What is this?" Stan asks. "Is it a gift?"

"I will not tell you," Tom winks at Stan.

Then he runs to the cab.

"This is my last task in West Trent," he yells as he jumps in the back of the cab. "And you must finish it."

"What task?" Stan yells.

"Just finish it for me!" Tom yells back as the cab sets off.

Next, the big red truck is off as well. Dust puffs up as the cab and the truck pass by Stan.

Chapter 3
Tom Has Left

Stan's mom preps lunch as he sprints by her.

"Stan!" she calls.

But Stan does not stop. He runs up the steps and hops on his bed. He still has the black tin chest in his hand.

"What is in this chest?" he thinks.

But he does not check it just yet. He thinks if he lifts the lid, he will admit that Tom has left.

He sets the chest on his desk. He sprints down the steps and bumps into his mom in the hall.

"Has Tom left?" she asks.

Stan nods.

His mom hugs him.

"I wish the stamp plant had not shut down," Stan sobs.

If the plant had not shut, Tom may not have left and Stan's dad may still have had a job.

"I wish that as well," says his mom, still hugging him.

Stan's mom grabs a glass.

"I will get you a drink." She fills the glass from the tap. "You have hash in the pot. Just have your dad crack an egg on top. Then you will be all set."

"Will you not have lunch with us?" asks Stan.

"I have a shift at the grill pub. Deb is sick and she is out."

"But Mom..." Stan grunts.

"An add-on shift helps a lot," she says.

She grabs her bag and runs out.

When the plant shut down, Stan's mom got a job at the grill pub. It is not a big job and the pay is not much. But it still helps with the bills.

So much is shifting so fast in West Trent. Stan does not like this a bit.

Chapter 4

The Black Tin Chest

Stan steps in the den with the glass in his hand. His dad is in the den with his laptop.

"Mom has left," he grunts.

His dad nods. He is still on his laptop checking the job ads.

Stan sits next to his dad. He checks what is on TV. He thinks a fun sitcom will help him stop thinking of Tom.

He clicks and clicks. There is not a fun thing on TV.

Fluff, Stan's cat, jumps on his lap. She rests on his chest. Stan hugs her as she naps.

Fluff was a gift to Stan from Gran Jenn.

"I wish Gran was still with us. She was the best," Stan thinks as he pats Fluff.

"Are there jobs for you, Dad?" he asks.

"No luck, Son," his dad shrugs. "Not just yet."

There is not much to do in West Trent.

Not for Stan.

Not for his dad.

Stan shuts off the TV. He does not wish to distract his dad so he gets a job as fast as he can.

With not much to do in the den, Stan runs up the steps. Fluff trots up next to him.

Stan sits on his bed. He picks up the tin chest from his desk.

The cat jumps next to him and licks the chest.

"No! Stop it, Fluff!" Stan snaps at the cat. "This is from Tom!"

Then he lifts the lid.

In the black tin chest, there is a map.

Chapter 5

Map In The Chest

Stan picks up the map. It has West Trent on it. He sets the map on his desk. Fluff hops on the desk and sniffs the map.

There is so much Stan must ask Tom.

Why is the map in the chest?

What is Tom's last task that Stan must finish?

Stan spots a big red X on the map at the bus stop next to the vet clinic.

"What will I do at the bus stop?" he thinks.

Stan grabs his cap and the map. He runs down the steps.

"I will be out for a bit, Dad!" he yells as he steps out. He sprints to the bus stop by the vet clinic. He checks the stop, but he cannot spot a thing.

Why has Tom sent him there? It is just a bus stop. Has Tom left a hint at the bus stop for him?

Stan sits on the bench and thinks for a bit. Then he spots a crack in the wall next to the bench. In it, there is a red tag. He runs to it and yanks it out. A map is on the tag!

"This must be the next hint," Stan thinks. "Tom is nuts!"

Stan does not check what is on this map. He has to go back to have the hash with his dad.

On the way back from the bus stop, Stan spots a cab at Mrs. Prim's.

Mrs. Prim was his gran's best pal. They led the quilt club in West Trent. Stan had a lot of fun with them.

A kid and her mom stand in front of Mrs. Prim's with lots of bags.

"Who can they be?" Stan thinks. "I think she is 12 just like me."

Chapter 6
Mrs. Prim's Grandkid

Stan gets back as his dad packs his laptop.

"There was a kid and her mom at Mrs. Prim's!" Stan tells his dad.

"I think they are Pam and her mom," says Stan's dad.

"Pam?" asks Stan in shock. "Pam as in Mrs. Prim's grandkid?"

His dad nods.

"Are they in from Grand Cliff?" Stan asks.

He cannot tell when Pam was in West Trent last.

"They must be in West Trent to visit Mrs. Prim," Stan's dad says.

He brings the pot and sets a big helping on Stan's dish.

"Dad, the eggs?"

"That is what I had to add!" Stan's dad gets a bit upset with himself.

"We can skip the eggs," Stan says. "Pam and her mom had lots of bags with them," he adds.

"Did you visit Mrs. Prim?" his dad asks.

"No, I was just at the bus stop," Stan says.

"Why were you at the bus stop?"

"Oh," says Stan. "This!"

He sets the maps in front of his dish.

"What is this?" his dad asks.

Stan tells his dad of Tom's gift as they finish lunch. He tells him of the tin chest and the maps.

"And this is the last map I got. It was at the bus stop," Stan says.

"The red X is at Mrs. Prim's. Do you think Pam can help you with the hint?" asks Stan's dad.

As of last spring when they lost Gran Jenn, Stan has not met up with Mrs. Prim at all. Stan felt as if she did not wish to visit him.

On top of that, he was mad at Mrs. Prim when she had quit the quilt club. He just did not get why she did that. So, he did not visit her at all.

Stan thinks having a pal to hang out with is not a bad plan. Yet, he does not stop by Mrs. Prim's to check the hint.

In the end, Stan just hangs out at the swing set with Fluff.

"Tom..." he thinks, "why did the hint have to be at Mrs. Prim's?"

Will Stan have the guts to visit Mrs. Prim's and get his hands on the next hint?

Chapter 7
A Visit To Mrs. Prim

"Get in, Pam!" says Mrs. Prim with a shrill. She is glad for this visit.

Pam steps in with her bag.

"When did you get this big?" Mrs. Prim hugs Pam. Then she adds, "Liz, so glad you got to West Trent O.K.!"

"Thank you, Mom!" Pam's mom, Liz, says. "Thanks for letting us stay with you."

Pam is not glad to be in West Trent. Her wish is to be back in Grand Cliff with her pals. There is not much in West Trent for her.

She gets that her mom is glad to be in West Trent. And it is O.K. to visit

Gran Prim for a bit. But Pam can tell this is not just a quick visit. She can tell they will not be back to Grand Cliff.

"I am glad you will stay with me," Mrs. Prim says as she hugs her.

Mrs. Prim grabs a bag.

"Is this all you have with you?" she asks.

Pam's mom nods.

"The rest will ship in a truck from Grand Cliff," she says as she picks up the rest of the bags.

They sit in the den and have drinks.

"Tell us, Mom. How are you?" Pam's mom asks.

"As well as I can be," says Mrs. Prim with a sad grin. "Just glad that you are in West Trent."

Then she picks up a box from next to the lamp.

"I got a gift for you, Pam." She hands Pam the box.

Pam unpacks the gift. It is a pink and black rug.

"This was my last rug at the quilt club." She pats the rug as if it is a pup. "You can have it next to your bed," she adds.

"Do you still run the quilt club?" Pam asks.

Mrs. Prim is glum.

"No. I just do not have it in me when Jenn is not there."

Pam is sad for Gran Prim. She lost her best pal, Jenn Kest, in the spring. In a way, Pam has lost her best pals as well. She left them in Grand Cliff and she has to be in West Trent with her mom and gran.

"But I can tell you that I must stop living in the past," adds Mrs. Prim.

That is when the bell rings.

Chapter 8
The Next Hint

Stan stands on Mrs. Prim's steps with the map in his hand.

"Stan!" Mrs. Prim runs to Stan and hugs him. "Has Tom left?"

Stan nods.

"I bet you must miss him," she adds.

She lets Stan in. "This is Pam. You met her when you were six, I think."

Pam does not say a thing.

"Can I get you a drink, Stan?" asks Pam's mom.

"No, thanks. But you can help with the map."

"Which map?" Mrs. Prim asks.

"Tom has left maps with hints on them. It was a map of the bus stop and then at the bus stop was this map."

Mrs. Prim checks the map.

"That is out back!" says Mrs. Prim.

"Can I check it out?" Stan asks.

"Yes," says Mrs. Prim. "Pam, can you help Stan?"

Pam shrugs.

Stan and Pam go to the back.

"Let us check the plant pots," Stan tells Pam.

He has a hunch the hint is in a pot.

Pam steps up to a big pot and picks it up. The hint is not there.

Stan lifts the pot next to it. No luck.

They check all the pots.

No chest.

No box.

No map.

No hints.

"Let us check the bench," Pam says.

Stan and Pam run to the bench.

Not a thing there.

They stand and think.

Then Pam yells, "The fish pond!"

She sprints to the pond and dips her hand in. She brings out a dripping wet ziplock bag.

"Yes!" Stan sits next to Pam. "What is in it?"

Pam splits the bag. A jug is in the bag. She tips the jug. But there is not a thing in it.

"We got a jug just like this in my class!" Stan jumps up. "It is on a shelf on the back wall in my class," he claps. "We must check the jug next!"

Chapter 9
The Sack In The Jug

The next day in class, the bell rings as Stan sits at his desk. Miss Kitts trots into the class with a kid next to her.

It is Pam.

"Class!" Miss Kitts claps her hands. "This is Pam Elm."

She brings Pam to the front of the class.

"Pam will be in this class. Help her fit in," Miss Kitts says. "Pam, you can sit next to Stan. That spot was Tom's. He has left West Trent and he will not be back."

Pam sits next to Stan and winks at him.

Stan grins. Then he nods at the back wall of the class. The jug stands on the shelf. A flag is in the jug.

Pam grins back. They must get up to the shelf!

Miss Kitts taps her pen on the desk.

"Check out Math Task 7," she tells the class.

Then she stops at the kids' desks to help them.

"Did you finish it, Pam?" she asks when she is next to her.

Pam nods.

"We did this in class back in Grand Cliff," she says.

All the kids rush out to lunch when the bell rings. But Pam and Stan do not get up. They hang at their desks until Miss Kitts steps out.

Then they go to the back of the class. Pam lifts her hand to the shelf on the wall, but she cannot grab the jug.

"I must stand on a desk!" Pam says.

Stan helps Pam bring the desk to the wall. Pam jumps on top. She picks up the jug and checks the flag.

The flag is not the next hint.

Then she sticks her hand in the jug.

"I got it!" she yells.

Chapter 10

The Napkin In The Sack

Pam grabs a sack with a string.

A red tag hangs on the string.

It says 'STAN' on it.

They bring the desk back to where it was. As they finish up, Miss Kitts steps back in the class to grab her handbag.

"Stan. Pam. You cannot be in class at lunch!"

Stan sticks the sack in his belt.

"Yes, Miss Kitts," he says as he runs out of the class with Pam.

They sprint out to where all the kids are. They sit on a big rock next to a shrub.

"What is in the sack?" asks Pam.

Stan brings out the sack and tips it. A napkin drops out.

The next hint is on the napkin. It is a big 'H' on top an 'H'. A red X is on the left of the 'H'.

"What can this 'H' be?" asks Pam with a thrill.

"I cannot think of an 'H' to go to!"

"Lunch will end in just a bit," says Pam. "Let us get a snack and a drink. It will help us think."

They grab a drink and chips. Then they go back to the rock.

When they finish, Stan asks Pam, "What brings you and your mom to West Trent?"

"Gran Prim," Pam says.

"But this is not just a quick trip, is it?" Stan squints.

"Mom got a job at the vet clinic," Pam nods. "She helps pets."

"Then I think your mom will like Fluff," Stan says.

"Fluff?" Pam asks.

"Fluff is my cat," Stan grins. "She is the best. If you pet her, she will lick your hand, like a pup. Tom has left and Fluff is all I have."

Pam nods.

"I wish I had a best pal in West Trent," she thinks. "Or a pet."

Just then the bell rings to end lunch.

Chapter 11
'H' Stands For

Stan's mom is at the pick up when class ends. Stan jumps in the van with a big grin.

He tells his mom that Pam is in his class and they got Tom's next hint in the jug.

"Well, then, you can crack Tom's hint with Pam. She can drop by," she tells Stan. "And her mom and Mrs. Prim as well," she adds.

"Can they?" Stan jumps up. "When, Mom?"

"Do you think a Sunday brunch will do?" Stan's mom checks her shift list from the grill pub. "I am off this Sunday."

"A brunch with Mrs. Prim!" Stan claps his hands. "Just as we did in the past."

"Yes," says his mom. "I will call Mrs. Prim to check if they can stop by. What do you think?"

"I think it is a grand plan!" Stan yells. "We can have eggs and ham. Mrs. Prim will like that the best."

"Eggs and ham it is," his mom says.

Stan picks up his backpack and gets out a pad and a pen. He jots down 'CALL MRS. PRIM FOR BRUNCH'. Then he hands it to his mom.

"To add to your to do list, Mom," he winks.

The sun has set. All day, Stan sat on the rug with the napkin in his lap. He still cannot think of what the 'H' can be.

The next day, Stan still thinks of the hint.

"What does this 'H' stand for?" Stan grunts. "Do you think 'H' will spell a thing?" he asks his dad sitting in the den with his laptop. "Where will I go next?"

Stan's dad shuts his laptop. He gets up and picks up the napkin.

"Well," he says. "When Tom was in West Trent, what did you do for fun?"

"Fishing," Stan says. "With rods. At the pond."

"No, that is not it," his dad says.

"Running?" asks Stan. "We ran a lot. On the track."

"I do not think it is the track."

"Tennis! At the club. With a net." Stan jumps up. "The net! That is it!"

His dad shrugs. "What are you getting at?"

Stan tilts the napkin to the left.

"The net!" he yells. "It is not an 'H'! The red X is next to the tennis net!"

Stan spins with his hands up. He is glad to crack the hint at last.

"That is it! The next hint must be at the tennis club. We must go get it, Dad!" he adds.

"It is 9:00 p.m." Stan's dad checks the clock. "Bath and then go to bed, Stan."

Chapter 12
The Brunch

The next day, Stan gets up with the sun. All he can think of is the tennis net, but his mom tells him to help her set up for brunch with Mrs. Prim, Pam and Pam's mom.

Stan gets Fluff a can of fish. Next, he helps his dad crack the eggs and cut the ham.

He checks the clock on the wall. It is just 10:30 a.m. He cannot get to the tennis club yet.

"When do we expect them?" he asks when he runs out of things to do.

"11 a.m.," his mom tells him.

Stan checks the clock.

It is 10:34.

Tick tock.

Tick tock.

Stan cannot sit still. He runs out to the swing set with Fluff.

He is glad that Pam, her mom and Mrs. Prim will stop by. This brunch will be the best.

He thinks back to when Mrs. Prim last met Stan for brunch. Gran Jenn was ill, but she still had a hand of Go Fish with Mrs. Prim and Stan. They let him win.

Just then, the bell rings. Stan and Fluff sprint back in. Stan runs up and stops next to his mom. But Fluff runs back out.

It is just Pam and her mom on the steps. Stan's mom lets them in.

"Where is Mrs. Prim?" Stan blasts. "Why is she not with you?"

Pam can tell Stan is upset.

"Stan!" his mom snaps. "What is up with you?"

Stan steps back.

"Gran Prim had to stay back," Pam says. "She felt a bit sick when she got up. You can check up on her if you wish, Stan."

Pam's mom hands Stan's mom a box. "This is a gift for you."

"Thank you!" Stan's mom says. "You did not have to."

Chapter 13

Mrs. Prim And Gran Jenn

Stan and Pam go out in the back as the moms stay in and get drinks.

Fluff sits on the wall next to the swing set.

"Is that Fluff?" asks Pam to get Stan to chat.

"Yes."

"Can I pet her?"

Stan nods. But he does not say much.

"Are you mad?" Pam asks.

Stan shrugs.

"Do you think you can trick me? I can tell you are mad. Are you not glad Mom and I are having brunch with you?" Pam asks.

Fluff jumps off the wall when she spots the kids and trots to them.

"I am glad," Stan says.

Fluff rubs her chin on Pam's legs. Pam bends and pats her. The cat licks Pam's hand.

"And Fluff is glad as well," Stan adds with a half grin. "It is just… I wish… Why is Mrs. Prim not having brunch with us?"

"She was not well," insists Pam. "You miss her, do you not?"

Stan nods.

"I think if she visits you, she thinks of your gran. She does miss her a lot," she adds.

Stan did not think of it that way. He did not think how Mrs. Prim must have felt when they lost Gran Jenn.

"How is she?" asks Stan.

"She is not that well," Pam says. "She still had plans to run the quilt club. But she had to quit it as well. I can tell it is not in her to go on with the club with no help."

Stan nods.

"Gran Jenn, Mrs. Prim and I did so much. It was the best. I lost my gran. But it is as if I lost Mrs. Prim as well." Stan says.

"You do not have to wish that she visits you. You can just visit her."

Pam is spot on. It was not just Mrs. Prim that held back. Stan held himself back as well.

Chapter 14
The Hint At The Club

Stan jumps up. "I did not tell you yet. I got the next spot for Tom's hint! We can check it when brunch ends."

"What is it?" Pam asks. "What did the 'H' spell?"

"It is not an 'H'. It is a tennis net! Well, I think it is. We must check it out."

Stan and Pam run back in when Stan's dad yells, "Kids, eggs and ham?"

They all grab a dish and sit down. Stan's dad hands out helpings of eggs and ham to the kids.

"Stan tells me you help pets?" Stan's dad hands a dish to Pam's mom. "What do you do?"

"Yes," says Pam's mom. "I am a vet. And I just got a job at the West Trent Pet Clinic."

"We bring Fluff to the clinic when she is sick and for her check-ups," Stan's mom tells her.

"And Mom says you had a job at the stamp plant," Pam's mom says to Stan's dad.

Stan shrinks.

Do they, in fact, have to bring up that his dad has no job when Pam sits next to him?

"Yes, I did. But the plant has shut down," Stan's dad says. "I am still on the hunt for a job."

"Best of luck," Pam's mom says.

Fluff jumps on Pam's lap.

"I think she is asking for a bit of ham," Stan's mom says.

Pam lets Fluff chomp on the last bit. Fluff gulps it down and then licks Pam's hand.

"Fluff says thank you," Stan grins.

When the kids finish their eggs and ham, Stan's dad lets them go to the tennis club.

Pam and Stan rush to the club. It is just six blocks down.

When they get to the club, Stan runs up to the net and grabs a black bag hanging from the net.

"I got it!" Stan yells.

He rips the bag. In it is a plastic bus.

"Is the next hint a bus?" asks Pam. "Or is it on a bus?"

"I bet the next hint is on a bus," Stan grins.

"But which bus?"

"It must be the bus to class. Tom sat on the back. That was his spot. It must be there," Stan grins. "We will have to crack this hint on Monday."

Chapter 15

Fluff Gets Sick

When the kids get back to Stan's, Pam and her mom go back to Mrs. Prim's.

Stan sits in the den. Fluff spots him and sits next to him. Stan thinks Fluff is sick.

"Mom, can you check on Fluff?" he asks.

"I cannot tell what is off with her," says his mom with a shrug. "But she is not well."

"You will be O.K.," Stan hums as he rubs Fluff's chin.

"Bring her to Pam's," his mom tells him. "Her mom can check up on her."

Stan picks Fluff up and runs as fast as he can to Pam's.

Pam sits up front with a pen and pad in her lap.

"What is up?" Pam asks.

"Fluff is sick," Stan says.

"I will get Mom."

Pam runs in and yells for her mom.

Mrs. Prim and Pam's mom rush out with Pam.

Stan hands Fluff to Pam's mom and runs to Mrs. Prim.

"Stan!" Mrs. Prim hugs him.

She is glad that Stan is there.

Stan hugs her back.

"Fluff is sick," Pam tells her mom.

Pam's mom checks the cat. "Stan, tell your mom to bring Fluff to the vet clinic."

"Is it bad?" Stan asks in a panic.

"Not at all," she hands Fluff back to Stan. "She must get a quick shot. That is it."

"How much is a shot?" Stan asks in a sad way. "Mom will not have funds for it just yet."

Pam cuts in. "Mom, can you do the shot? Then they will not have to pay?"

"Yes," Pam's mom says. "I am glad to. Stan, just tell your mom to ask for Liz Elm when she gets to the clinic."

Chapter 16

A Box From Madrid

At lunch the next day, Pam gets a text back from her mom.

Stan sits with his pals for lunch. Pam runs up to him.

Stan is glad that she stops by. "Pam, will you have lunch with us?"

"Can I chat with you for a sec?" she asks.

She does not spot the rest of the gang next to Stan.

But Eric butts in. "We have not met yet. You must be Pam," he stands up. "I am Eric. And this is Ann and Sid. We are the tennis gang."

They all nod.

Pam grins, then she bends down to Stan, "Can we chat for a bit?"

Stan stands up and they go out.

"Mom did the check-up and says Fluff is O.K.," Pam tells him.

"Yes, I got a text from Dad as well. Mom did not pay for the visit and the shot. Your mom is the best!"

"She was glad to help," Pam says. "I will let you go back in. You must finish your lunch."

"Sit with us," Stan says as they go back in to the lunch hall.

Pam grins and sits with Stan and the tennis gang.

When class ends, Pam stops by Stan's to check on Fluff.

"Fluff!" Pam hugs the cat. "I am glad you are O.K." She pats Fluff on the back.

"Where is Dad?" Stan asks his mom.

"He is out. He had a thing to do," his mom tells him. "Stan, you got a box from Tom!" she adds.

"From Tom?" Stan yells with a shrill.

He picks it up from the desk and rips off the top. He checks the things that Tom has sent.

"What is in the box?" Pam asks.

"A lot of Spanish stuff," Stan yells with a shrill. "I miss him a lot!"

"Oh," Pam says. She is sad. "Do you wish Tom was in West Trent and I was in Grand Cliff?"

"I wish Tom was back, but I wish you to stay in West Trent as well. You and Tom are my best pals," Stan tells her. "I have a best pal in Madrid and a best pal in West Trent."

Pam is glad for that.

She checks the box Stan left on the desk.

"What is that?" she asks.

"It is a tag." Stan picks it up. "It says: 4 – 7 – 2 – 5. FOR THE LOCK."

"The lock?" Pam shrugs.

"We did not check the bus! I let that slip when Fluff got sick. Tom's last hint was a plastic bus. There must be a lock on the bus."

Chapter 17

A Job For Stan's Dad

Just then, Stan's dad is back.

"I got the job!" he sings from the hall.

A job!

Pam and Stan jump up.

Stan runs to his dad and hugs him.

Then he stops and asks, "Dad, will we have to go for your job like Tom had to. Will we?"

"Oh, no!" Stan's dad says. "The job is just 30 min from West Trent. We can stay where we are."

"I am glad for that," Stan says. "Check this out, Dad. Tom sent a box."

"This is the best day! Let us grill fish and have fun," says Stan's mom.

"Go get your mom and Mrs. Prim," Stan's dad tells Pam. "They must be with us as well. Be quick."

Pam runs out and is back in a flash with her mom and Mrs. Prim.

Pam and Stan sit on the grass. The rest sit next to the grill. They all get drinks.

Fluff smells the fish on the grill. He trots up to beg for a bit of the fish.

Pam sets down her drink and picks up the cat.

"We must get a pic of all of us," says Stan's mom to Mrs. Prim. "I will print it out and send it to you with Stan."

"I must tell all of you," Stan's dad says. "I am glad I got a job!"

"Things are all well at last," Pam's mom says.

"Yes, it is," says Mrs. Prim, "for all of us. And I think we can all drink to that," she adds as she lifts her glass.

They all lift their drinks.

Chapter 18
The Lockbox

The next day, Stan jots 4 – 7 – 2 – 5 on the back of his hand and then runs to the bus stop. It is 7:00 a.m.

Pam gets to the stop at 7:05. But it is still 10 min until they expect the bus to be at the stop.

"Do you think this is the bus that Tom left the hint on," asks Pam.

"I bet it is," Stan grins.

Pam brings out snacks from her bag.

"A bag of chestnuts," Stan yelps. "That is the best snack."

Pam nods with a grin. "Dig in, if you wish."

They chomp on chestnuts until the bus is at the stop.

There is a lot of traffic. The bus gets to the stop at 7:20. The kids jump on and run to the back of the bus. Stan sits in Tom's spot. He sticks his hand in the gap.

There it is. It is a box with a lock on it.

"Quick!" says Pam. "Unlock the box!"

Stan checks the back of this hand.

He plugs $4 - 7 - 2 - 5$ on the lock pad.

The box clicks and unlocks.

Stan flips the lid up.

Chapter 19
Tom's Last Task

"What is in the box?" Pam asks. "Tell me!"

Stan brings out a stack of prints.

"Tom and me..."

There are a lot of them, all with Tom and Stan.

"This is us at the tennis club. We were ten back then."

Stan prods Pam with a big grin.

"Check this out, Pam. This is when we went swimming in the pond. We had a lot of fun."

Stan is glad for this gift.

"Did I tell you that I met Tom?" asks Pam.

Stan stops grinning.

"You met Tom? When?" he asks in shock.

"Tom had a chat with my mom when we were in Grand Cliff. He set this all up. We had a quick stop at the tennis club and met with Tom and his mom and dad. It was the day we got to West Trent. And they were in a cab with all their stuff."

Stan is still in shock.

"Are you mad that I did not tell you this?" asks Pam.

Stan still flips the prints. Then he stops. "I bet this was Tom's epic plan."

"Yes, it was his plan," Pam adds, "to tell us that he left a hint at Gran

Prim's. He did not tell us what he was up to. He did not let us check what he did. I just had to help you if and when you stop by. Is that not odd?"

"This is the last task I had to finish." Stan taps his chin for a bit. "Tom is the best!"

"The last task?" Pam squints.

"Tom has a gift for such things," Stan grins. "He got me to stop by Mrs. Prim and hang out with her. Plus, we got to be pals as we hunt for the hints he left."

Then he jumps up as he yells, "Just hang on a sec!"

He checks his backpack. He picks up a print. It is Pam and Stan when they were grilling at Stan's.

"We must add this to the stack," he says. "Let us do lots of fun things as well. Just like Tom and I did."

"As if we are best pals?"

"We ARE best pals!" Stan fist bumps Pam and grins. "What do you think of West Trent?"

"Well," Pam grins, "still not much to do. But a best pal like you brings out the best in West Trent."

You can download full color

CERTIFICATE OF ACCOMPLISHMENT
and
CERTIFICATE OF COMPLETION

on our website

SIMPLEWORDSBOOKS.COM

Certificate of Accomplishment

This certificate is awarded to

_____

for successful completion of

The Last Task

_____
Signature

_____
Date

THE LAST TASK
WORD LIST

#	Word	Count	#	Word	Count	#	Word	Count
1	a	166	26	be	33	51	by	11
2	a.m.	3	27	bed	4	52	cab	9
3	add	3	28	beds	1	53	call	3
4	add-on	1	29	beg	1	54	calls	1
5	adds	13	30	bell	5	55	can	39
6	admit	1	31	belt	1	56	cannot	9
7	ads	1	32	bench	4	57	cap	1
8	all	26	33	bends	2	58	cat	8
9	am	10	34	best	24	59	chat	4
10	an	6	35	bet	4	60	check	21
11	and	132	36	big	13	61	checking	1
12	Ann	1	37	bills	1	62	checks	13
13	are	24	38	bit	12	63	check-up	1
14	as	47	39	black	5	64	check-ups	1
15	ask	2	40	blasts	1	65	chest	12
16	asking	1	41	block	1	66	chestnuts	2
17	asks	43	42	blocks	1	67	chin	4
18	at	47	43	box	13	68	chips	1
19	Atlantic	1	44	bring	7	69	chomp	2
20	back	45	45	brings	10	70	claps	3
21	backpack	3	46	brunch	9	71	class	18
22	bad	2	47	bumps	2	72	clicks	3
23	bag	10	48	bus	26	73	Cliff	8
24	bags	4	49	but	29	74	clinic	7
25	bath	1	50	butts	1	75	clock	3

#	Word	Count	#	Word	Count	#	Word	Count
76	club	14	101	egg	1	126	fun	9
77	crack	6	102	eggs	8	127	funds	1
78	cut	1	103	Elm	2	128	gang	3
79	cuts	1	104	end	3	129	gap	1
80	dad	57	105	ends	3	130	get	23
81	dads	1	106	epic	1	131	gets	12
82	day	10	107	Eric	2	132	getting	1
83	Deb	1	108	expect	2	133	gift	8
84	den	6	109	fact	1	134	glad	20
85	desk	11	110	fall	2	135	glass	4
86	desks	2	111	fast	4	136	glum	1
87	did	29	112	felt	3	137	go	24
88	dig	1	113	fills	1	138	got	21
89	dips	1	114	finish	10	139	grab	4
90	dish	4	115	fish	6	140	grabs	7
91	distract	1	116	fishing	1	141	gran	17
92	do	33	117	fist	1	142	grand	9
93	does	12	118	fit	1	143	grandkid	1
94	down	13	119	flag	3	144	grass	3
95	drink	6	120	flash	1	145	grill	6
96	drinks	4	121	flips	2	146	grilling	1
97	dripping	1	122	Fluff	41	147	grin	6
98	drop	1	123	for	45	148	grinning	1
99	drops	2	124	from	20	149	grins	12
100	dust	1	125	front	5	150	grunts	4

#	Word	Count	#	Word	Count	#	Word	Count
151	gulps	1	176	himself	2	201	jots	2
152	guts	1	177	hint	22	202	jug	10
153	H	11	178	hints	3	203	jump	2
154	had	22	179	his	78	204	jumps	12
155	half	2	180	hops	2	205	just	32
156	hall	3	181	hot	1	206	Kest	1
157	ham	7	182	how	4	207	kicks	1
158	hand	13	183	hug	1	208	kid	3
159	handbag	1	184	hugging	1	209	kids	9
160	hands	12	185	hugs	10	210	Kitts	7
161	hang	4	186	hums	1	211	lamp	1
162	hanging	1	187	hunch	1	212	lap	4
163	hangs	2	188	hunt	2	213	laptop	5
164	has	24	189	hush	1	214	last	15
165	hash	2	190	I	87	215	led	1
166	have	28	191	if	14	216	left	17
167	having	3	192	ill	1	217	legs	1
168	he	114	193	in	119	218	let	12
169	held	2	194	insists	1	219	lets	4
170	help	12	195	into	2	220	letting	1
171	helping	1	196	is	165	221	lick	1
172	helpings	1	197	it	96	222	licks	3
173	helps	5	198	Jenn	8	223	lid	5
174	her	59	199	job	21	224	lift	2
175	him	26	200	jobs	4	225	lifts	5

#	Word	Count
226	like	9
227	list	2
228	living	2
229	Liz	3
230	lock	5
231	lost	9
232	lot	12
233	lots	3
234	luck	3
235	lunch	12
236	mad	4
237	Madrid	5
238	map	17
239	maps	3
240	math	1
241	may	3
242	me	13
243	men	2
244	met	7
245	min	2
246	miss	14
247	mom	84
248	moms	1
249	Monday	1
250	Mrs.	50

#	Word	Count
251	much	11
252	must	26
253	my	8
254	napkin	5
255	naps	1
256	net	8
257	next	44
258	no	15
259	nod	1
260	nods	14
261	not	81
262	nuts	1
263	O.K.	5
264	odd	1
265	of	52
266	off	9
267	oh	3
268	on	70
269	or	3
270	out	38
271	p.m.	2
272	packs	1
273	pad	3
274	pal	9
275	pals	8

#	Word	Count
276	Pam	137
277	panic	1
278	pass	1
279	past	3
280	pats	4
281	pay	3
282	pen	3
283	pet	4
284	pets	2
285	pic	1
286	pick	1
287	picks	13
288	pink	1
289	plan	7
290	plans	1
291	plant	11
292	plastic	2
293	plugs	1
294	plus	1
295	pond	4
296	pot	5
297	pots	2
298	preps	1
299	Prim	55
300	print	2

#	Word	Count
301	prints	2
302	prods	1
303	pub	3
304	puffs	1
305	pup	2
306	quick	7
307	quilt	5
308	quit	2
309	ran	1
310	red	9
311	rest	4
312	rests	1
313	rings	5
314	rips	2
315	rock	3
316	rods	1
317	rubs	2
318	rug	4
319	run	5
320	running	1
321	runs	20
322	rush	4
323	sack	4
324	sad	6
325	sags	1

#	Word	Count
326	sat	2
327	say	3
328	says	64
329	sec	2
330	send	1
331	sent	3
332	set	10
333	sets	6
334	she	85
335	shelf	4
336	shift	3
337	shifting	1
338	ship	2
339	shock	3
340	shot	4
341	shrill	3
342	shrinks	1
343	shrub	1
344	shrug	1
345	shrugs	5
346	shut	6
347	shuts	2
348	sick	7
349	Sid	1
350	sings	1

#	Word	Count
351	sit	10
352	sitcom	1
353	sits	15
354	sitting	1
355	six	2
356	skip	1
357	slip	1
358	smells	1
359	snack	2
360	snacks	1
361	snaps	2
362	sniffs	2
363	so	7
364	sobs	1
365	son	1
366	Spanish	2
367	spell	2
368	spins	1
369	splits	1
370	spot	7
371	spots	5
372	spring	3
373	sprint	2
374	sprints	4
375	squints	2

#	Word	Count	#	Word	Count	#	Word	Count
376	stack	2	401	tells	19	426	tock	2
377	staff	1	402	ten	1	427	Tom	67
378	stamp	4	403	tennis	11	428	top	6
379	stan	230	404	text	2	429	track	2
380	stand	4	405	thank	3	430	traffic	1
381	stands	6	406	thanks	2	431	Trent	30
382	stay	7	407	that	45	432	trick	1
383	steps	14	408	the	330	433	trip	1
384	sticks	3	409	their	8	434	trots	4
385	still	20	410	them	11	435	truck	7
386	stop	28	411	then	30	436	trunk	1
387	stops	9	412	there	21	437	TV	4
388	string	2	413	they	46	438	unlock	1
389	stuff	4	414	thing	8	439	unlocks	1
390	stuffs	1	415	things	6	440	unpacks	1
391	such	1	416	think	24	441	until	3
392	sun	3	417	thinking	1	442	up	51
393	Sunday	2	418	thinks	16	443	upset	2
394	swimming	1	419	this	46	444	us	20
395	swing	4	420	thrill	1	445	van	1
396	tag	6	421	tick	2	446	vet	5
397	tap	1	422	tilts	1	447	visit	10
398	taps	2	423	tin	5	448	visits	2
399	task	6	424	tips	2	449	wall	8
400	tell	20	425	to	157	450	was	33

#	Word	Count
451	way	5
452	we	37
453	well	22
454	went	1
455	were	6
456	West	30
457	wet	1
458	what	32
459	when	35
460	where	6
461	which	2
462	who	1
463	why	7
464	will	40
465	win	1
466	winks	3
467	wish	18
468	with	76
469	X	4
470	yanks	1
471	yells	15
472	yelps	1
473	yes	13
474	yet	8
475	you	97

#	Word	Count
476	your	14
477	ziplock	1
Total Words		**6001**

Do you want to write your own story now?

Written by: _____

_____

_____

_____

_____

_____

_____

_____

_____

_____

_____

_____

_____

_____

_____

_____

_____

_____

_____

_____

_____

_____

Do you want to draw your own story now?

Illustrated by:

WANT TO READ
MORE
CHAPTER BOOKS

STUDY GUIDES
AND
HANDBOOKS

www.simplewordsbooks.com

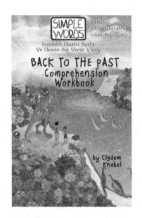

SIMPLE WORDS
Fluency · Comprehension · Self-Confidence
Decodable Chapter Books
We Choose Our Words Wisely

BACK TO THE PAST
Comprehension Workbook

by Cigdem Knebel

SIMPLE WORDS
Fluency · Comprehension · Self-Confidence
Decodable Chapter Books
We Choose Our Words Wisely

Spelling Pen
Red Obelisk

Comprehension Workbook

by C.Knebel

SIMPLE WORDS
Fluency · Comprehension · Self-Confidence
Decodable Chapter Books
We Choose Our Words Wisely

Spelling Pen in Elf Land
Comprehension Workbook

by C.Knebel

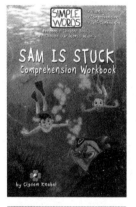

SIMPLE WORDS
Fluency · Comprehension · Self-Confidence
Decodable Chapter Books
We Choose Our Words Wisely

SAM IS STUCK
Comprehension Workbook

by Cigdem Knebel

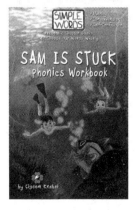

SIMPLE WORDS
Fluency · Comprehension · Self-Confidence
Decodable Chapter Books
We Choose Our Words Wisely

SAM IS STUCK
Phonics Workbook

by Cigdem Knebel

SIMPLE WORDS
Fluency · Comprehension · Self-Confidence
Decodable Chapter Books
We Choose Our Words Wisely

FOX HUNT
Comprehension Workbook

by Cigdem Knebel

VISIT OUR WEBSITE FOR FREE RESOURCES

simplewordsbooks.com

AND CHECK OUT OUR FREE ONLINE SUMMITS